IMAGES
of America

SANTA PAULA
1930–1960

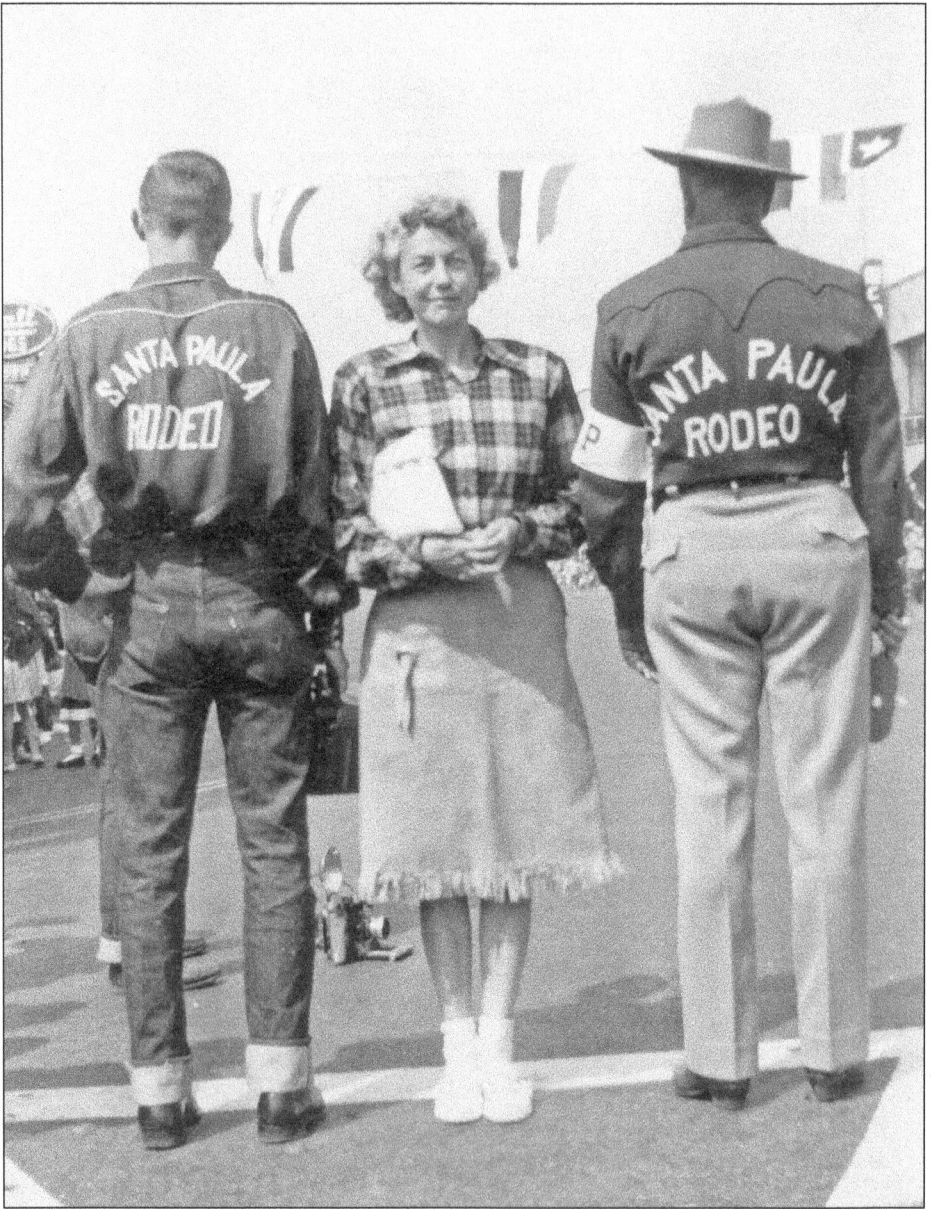

EARLY ADVERTISEMENT. This was one of the more unique ways to advertise one of the city's most popular annual events. Names of the participants are unknown.

ON THE COVER: The city's first newspaper, the *Santa Paula Chronicle*, rolled off the press in 1886 as a weekly. Fifty years later, it was a six-day-a-week periodical with evening home delivery. Thursday was the advertisements edition, and local merchants' full-page advertisements promoted eye-stopping bargains. Stores were open late on Saturdays to accommodate all; generally none but small neighborhood stores were open on Sundays. The editor-publisher was Leo A. Smith. He assumed ownership in mid-1924 and held the helm for many years. Like all previous predecessors, his *Chronicle* remained a Republican newspaper. Pictured from left to right are A. B. Veale, R. H. Jamison, Ed Lawrence, Nellie Bercaw, Warren L. King, H. A. Cheek, William Reese, F. J. Palmer, and Mildred Coombs. (Photograph courtesy of John Nichols Gallery.)

IMAGES
of America

SANTA PAULA
1930–1960

Mary Alice Orcutt Henderson

ARCADIA
PUBLISHING

Published by Arcadia Publishing
Charleston, South Carolina

Library of Congress Control Number: 2009932659

For all general information contact Arcadia Publishing at:
Telephone 843-853-2070
Fax 843-853-0044
E-mail sales@arcadiapublishing.com
For customer service and orders:
Toll-Free 1-888-313-2665

Visit us on the Internet at www.arcadiapublishing.com

This book is dedicated to those descendants of the pioneering families and those who came later, who built upon the strong foundation that their parents bequeathed them. You have left an incredible legacy that we must all strive to enhance for the next generation to inherit.

CONTENTS

ACKNOWLEDGMENTS

Credit goes to Arcadia Publishing for encouraging me to write this sequel, for without it there would have been no way to illustrate, through pictures and through captions, the important part that Mexican immigrants and Americans of Mexican descent played in the further development of Santa Paula. Even though the book's content was limited by the quality and quantity of photographs loaned, I hope that those presented are sufficient to show that the city's continued achievements reflected the contributions of all of its citizens.

Recently the Blanchard Community Library and the Santa Paula Historical Society jointly funded the transferring of over 100 years of *Santa Paula Chronicles* to a digitized format. This was a timely modernization that eased the tedium of researching specific news items more than words can tell.

The public solicitation for family pictures resulted in nearly 1,000 images from over 100 contributors—unfortunately, too many to list individually. However, those images not used are to be archived in the Santa Paula Historical Society's impressive historic photograph collection for future use and as research resources. One person, who is also one very good friend, I must acknowledge by name is Angela Huerta Preciado Dominguez. Without her pushing and prodding of family and friends, the book's interest and diversity would be severely lacking. Thanks also to Officer Carlos Juarez for securing unique photographs from the Santa Paula Police Department's records.

As always, I am grateful to my older brother Bill Orcutt for his input and editing; my youngest daughter, Anne Henderson, for her invaluable assistance in collating the photographs and captions into the final product; and to my excellent "scan man," Les Amman, for again giving the pictures premium attention for minimum remuneration.

In conclusion, the author expresses appreciation to all who shared their photographs, offered their historic tidbits or personal anecdotes to add to the captions, and provided expressions of encouragement. It has been a most interesting and rewarding experience.

INTRODUCTION

This is the sequel to the book that spanned Santa Paula's first 50 years—a formative, yet tentative, period when the pioneering settlers experimented with various produce to find the ideal cash crop and searched for the illusive sources of petroleum to develop a field. Eventually their efforts led to a telling discovery. Citrus cultivation became their orange ore; oil production their black gold. These are the two industries upon which the town built its foundation and which guaranteed its cityhood.

The first book focused more on the development of those industries; the impact the "coming of the railroad" had on fast-tracking the town to a promising future; the evolution of its Main Street from temporary buildings to permanent structures. It also showed the transition of individual families into a collective community of schools, churches, and neighborhoods.

Reflecting upon the local and national events that affected the city over the ensuing 30 years, the author chose this time to concentrate more on the people and how they lived. It must be remembered that the history told is limited to the variety of photographs shared for the project. Understandably, there are no images of how families managed or struggled during the Depression years. Why memorialize hard times? The exceptions were their weddings.

The largest chapter is devoted to their military service. Again, considering by 1942 over 400 men and women from Santa Paula were serving in the armed services, the number of photographs given was small but extremely important and valued. The second-largest chapter focuses on how they spent their leisure times and celebrated their good times. Incorporated in this section are a few pictures hinting of Santa Paula's historic association with well-known artists.

One

MAIN STREET
1930s

SANTA PAULA. The population was 7,395 exactly (according to the 1930 census). There were 11 churches of various denominations, one day nursery, three grammar schools, one junior high, and one Union High School. Industries included seven fruit and nut packinghouses, one lima bean warehouse, several automobile agencies, Union Oil of California, plus a half-dozen independent petroleum companies and one small oil refinery. Main Street's central business core ran from Eighth to Eleventh Streets and offered everything from antimacassars to zippers. Among the prominent public buildings were city hall, County Agricultural Commissioner's Office, Ebell Clubhouse, Glen Tavern Hotel, the library, and the Southern Pacific Depot. Though no longer on the main line, both freight and passenger trains were as regular as clockwork. This photograph was taken from McKevett Heights Hill. (Photograph courtesy of John Nichols Gallery.)

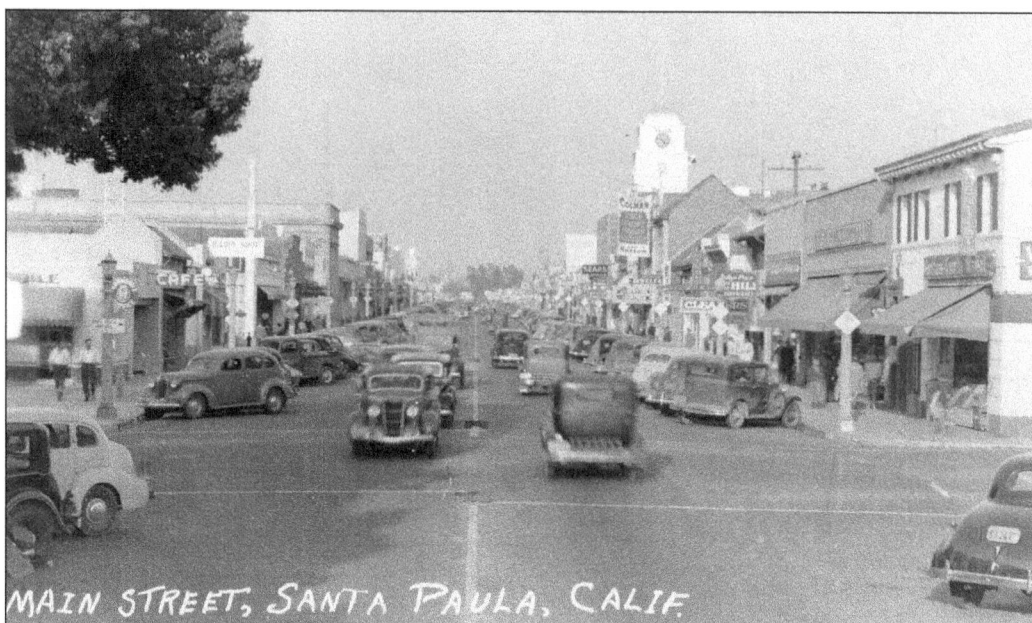

MAIN STREET, SANTA PAULA, CALIF.

MAIN AND EIGHTH STREETS INTERSECTION. Were one able to climb to the same height today and look eastward, too, there would be no significant difference in the buildings themselves. Just built is the two-story structure on the right known as the H. I. Q. Brown Building. A Roy Wilson design, the first floor housed a grocery, with the primary occupant of the second floor being Dr. Brown and his dental offices.

CITIZENS STATE BANK. In 1937, the Main Street landmark received its first and only face-lift. While the original building materials were masked, local architect Bob Raymond fortunately preserved this original arched entryway of locally quarried Sespe brownstone, which was complemented by the slender columns of green Catalina Serpentine. Also preserved was the institution's public statement: "Community owned, community minded."

BANK OF AMERICA. Located on the opposite corner of Citizens State Bank, this institution's name reflected the recent merger of the Bank of America of California with the Bank of Italy. The new bank assumed building, employees, and customers of the previous occupant.

THE FINAL PIECE. Sited on the primary intersection of Main and Tenth Streets, the completion of this building marked the removal of the last wooden structure along the main thoroughfare. The original occupant was C. C. Rupert's place of business, which offered stationery, office supplies, pictures, paintings, framing, and once-a-week art lessons. (Photograph courtesy of John Nichols Gallery.)

MAJOR RESTORATION. In the mid-1930s, the old Fulwieler's Garage on Main Street was transformed into an up-to-date grocery. The term "super" on the sign meant that various departments were consolidated into one store so that the lady of the house need only to stop and shop here for all her cooking requirements. Owner George Pezold was an avid promoter of his grocery and his city.

WARREN KING BUILDING. A Main Street fire destroyed four businesses, one of which belonged to fire chief Warren King and which was one of the first to be reopened, refurbished, and restocked. In appreciation of his volunteer fire department, he held a special "Firemen's Ball" with a 12-piece orchestra and a hardwood floor for dancing. The motto "Where quality is higher than price" guaranteed the furniture store's popularity.

SANTA PAULA INN HOTEL. Although the photograph dates later, the venerable lodging dates to the early 1900s. Catty-corner to the depot, it had a clientele that tended toward the working class. An advertisement from the 1930s declared it was "clean, restful and homelike, hot and cold running water," too!

THE COUNTY'S FIRST. This was Ventura County's first fire station and was built adjoining the County Agricultural Commissioner's office at the corner of Santa Barbara and Eighth Streets. Within a few years, other county-operated stations appeared throughout the county.

THE RAIN BEGAN. A warm storm brought the first drops on February 27, 1938. Showers became downpours. By the next day, between 2 and 4 inches had fallen. A brief break was followed by a second, more powerful storm with strong winds. Another 4 inches fell within 24 hours. Emergency crews evacuated 50 families from an area shown here, south of Harvard Boulevard. (Photograph courtesy of John Nichols Gallery.)

WILLARD BRIDGE, MARCH 2, 1938. The flooding Santa Clara River ripped out the connecting span at Twelfth Street. Main bridges throughout the valley fared no better. River and creek crossings were impossible. The dangling pipelines carrying crude oil from the South Mountain fields burst into flames, adding to the anxiety of an already anxious volunteer fire department. The city sanitation officer reported that 1,500 people were left homeless.

Temporary Transportation over the Roaring Waters. Southern California Edison employees rigged a "bull line" to haul stranded students, oil workers, and needed supplies across the flooding Santa Clara River. The cautionary words "just hold tight and don't look down" made the journey across in the swaying 55-gallon oil drum even more thrilling or exceedingly frightening.

CCC Boys to the Rescue. Some 125 young men from the nearby California Conservation Corps Camp came to Santa Paula to assist in flood protection and later with clean-up. Their welcomed assistance was provided without cost. The photograph could be titled, "Come Hell or High Water," as a cadre of men laid sandbag berms to protect the railroad line.

HAROLD B. SKILLIN MORTUARY. Designed by local architect Roy Wilson Sr. and located in a prominent neighborhood, the exterior reflects the new trend of creating a residence-like funeral home. As requested by the civic-minded owner, it was imperative that only local craftsmen be employed whenever possible. The adjoining church-like structure is the Memory Chapel and continues to be very popular for non-secular services.

MURAL. The focal point of the Memory Chapel is this mural painted by local artists Jessie Arms and Cornelis Botke. It was designed by Botke, who was inspired by a biblical passage to portray the promise of eternal life by painting the mighty eucalyptus trees reaching toward the heavens. He chose muted shades of greens and pinks to create this lovely setting of peaceful solitude, measuring approximately 21 by 24 feet.

MASTERCRAFT LAUNDERERS. After the establishment of this laundry in the early 1920s, the expansion of the oil industry increased its list of customers. The company's delivery trucks traveled weekly as far afield as Bakersfield, Taft, and Santa Maria and points in between. For locals, they advertised the laundering services of "Finish, Rough Dry, Damp Wash, and Permutit Soft Water." Their slogan—"A laundry does it best!"—is repeated in the building's six small signs. (Photograph courtesy of John Nichols Gallery.)

A FAIR EXCHANGE. A few months earlier, this proud early morning angler, Dick Dunbar, was a baker living in Iowa. When he spotted an advertisement from a baker in Santa Paula, California, wanting to trade his business for one in Iowa, Dunbar jumped at the chance. Moving lock, stock, and flour barrel with wife and children, he painted the name of his new concern boldly on his delivery truck.

Shoe Repair Shop. Located on Main Street in a downstairs corner room of the Union Oil building, Central Shoes offered half soles and heel caps of leather or rubber. Posing behind the counter on the left is the proprietor, Manual Victoria, with his brother Salvador. The Main Street presence of a Victoria shoe repair was resumed with his son Jess and remained a popular business and gathering place for years.

Watkins Hardware Company. As an existing business relocating to Main Street, owner Bob Watkins expressed confidence that the new location would serve both he and his loyal customers well. He was right, for the store lasted a long time. The photograph shows that his floor displays were stocked with a variety of items to appeal to all ages, all genders, and all year.

Two

MAIN STREET
1940s

MAIN AND DAVIS STREETS. Looking eastward, on the left is Farmers and Merchants Bank and, farther down, McMahans Furniture, which had acquired the old King Furniture business. On the right are two new names, Sears Roebuck and the 5-10-15 Cent Store. Over the Sears store is the Hotel Marion. The other two-story buildings are Balcom Hall (left) and Citizens State Bank (right). (Photograph courtesy of John Nichols Gallery.)

STORE ON EAST MAIN STREET. George Harding assumed ownership of the previous owner's building and stock of furniture. Harding added the adjective "Used" to his sign, believing there was a need for quality new and secondhand furniture in his hometown. His hunch proved correct. An only-in-a-small-town happenstance was this: his father-in-law was Warren King, owner of the popular King Furniture, which carried only new furnishings.

LA HACIENDA. Ruby Dominguez Carrillo Cárdenas poses in front of her café. Located on East Main Street, her business served Mexican food and offered a bar. (Photograph courtesy of John Nichols Gallery.)

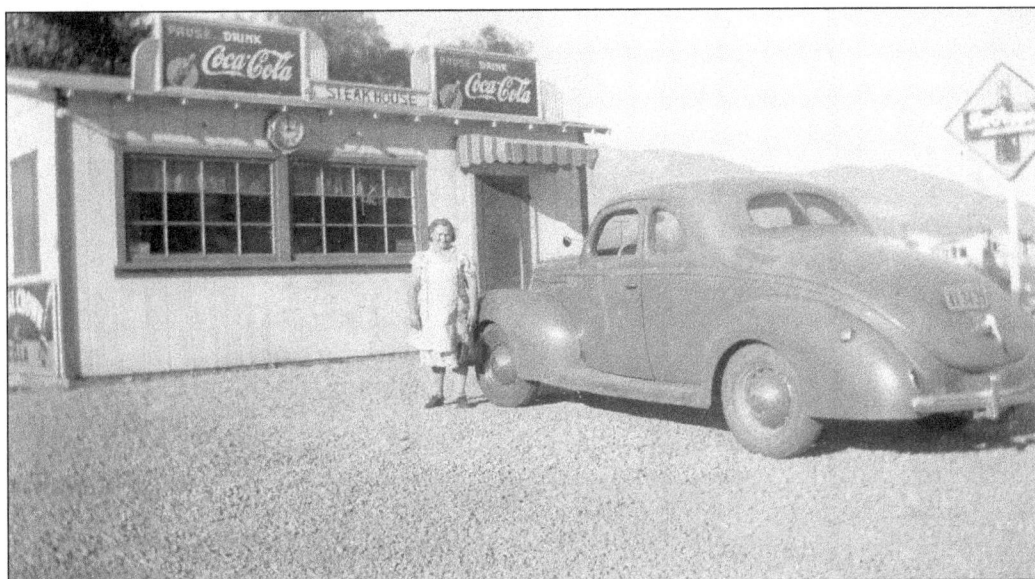

HARVARD BOULEVARD EATERY. Owner and chef Margaret Hill poses in front of her place known simply as the Steak House. Since she catered to the oil field workers, no doubt the menu was heavy on meat and potatoes and always offered homemade pies.

STEAK HOUSE'S KITCHEN. With the able assistance of waitress Martha Campen, Hill managed to serve up platters of steaks and all the trimmings in these very cramped quarters. The sign on the wall said it all, "The finest people in the world come here—our customers."

VENTURA COUNTY MARKET. Relocated from their Eighth and Main Streets corner, the Jue brothers, Joe, Jake, and Herbert (with cousin Walton), opened their store in this new building at 116 South Mill Street in October 1945. Designed by architect Roy Wilson Sr., in addition to state-of-the-art refrigeration, the modern market offered key features such as the concrete walls and floors. An added bonus for shoppers was the offered S&H Green Stamps.

DURING THE WAR. Since it was wartime, rationing and the "less days" (no sugar, no flour, no meat) severely limited available products for the consumers. Such federal government mandates ensured that sufficient staples and meat were available for the armed forces. At the time, Ventura County Market was the largest independent market in the county.

AFTER THE WAR. In anticipation of the resumption of available produce, products, and essentials, the owners had their market refurbished with new shelving and better lighting and restocked with a variety of items. They also changed the name to Jue's Market, which served loyal customers well into the 1970s.

SANTA PAULA TAXI. Clara Behrens, shown here, and her husband, Harold, initially owned just the taxi business, which included three cabs working out of 104 North Mill Street. The neighboring businesses were the Greyhound Bus Depot and Western Union. Eventually the Behrenses acquired them, too. Harold and two other drivers manned the taxis; Clara handled the books as well as the dispatching, reservations, and sending/receiving responsibilities of each service.

NO FATALITIES. This horrific accident occurred at the corner of A Street and old Highway 126 in Fillmore. The flattened car had been stolen in Santa Paula. The cab was turning the corner when the speeding vehicle slammed into it broadside with such force that it was spun completely around. Bob Buffalo, the cabby, said the driver leaped out and fled. The unidentified thief was never found, and Buffalo recovered.

CITY OFFICIALS AND STAFF. Pictured from left to right are (first row) Erbie Wilson, unidentified, fire chief Sam Primmer, Barbara Mosher Harrington, Tess Price, and ? Rhodes; (second row) Bob Crumrine, Frank Engledow, Horace Dowell, Grant Mickel, police captain Tom Moore, and unidentified; (third row) Edith Fandre, Thelma Minor, Agnes ?, Judge Alice Magill, unidentified sheriff's deputy, and sheriff's deputy Perry Barker.

IT'S WARTIME, 1943. Men of the Santa Paula Volunteer Fire Department pose in front of the firehouse wearing their Civil Defense helmets. From left to right are (kneeling) N. K. Lincoln, Frank Mosher, unidentified, and Leonard Phinney; (standing) Joe Wellman, Herman Rounds, P. A. Giacomazzi, Steve Love, George Harding, Everett Morrison, Chief Warren King, Jack Singleton, and Norman Lair.

A POPULAR MAN. Driver Ray Holts and his family lived in Santa Paula. He delivered Coca-Cola to both his hometown and the neighboring communities for over 20 years. His customers included neighborhood groceries and supermarkets, cafés and restaurants, and all gas stations that displayed the ubiquitous red metal refrigerated fixture always chock-full of ice-cold Cokes.

A GRAND PRIZE. George Pezold (right), as the owner of Santa Paula Super Market, enjoyed sponsoring contests as much as he did selling groceries. He regularly offered drawings for a variety of items to help the lady of the house. On this occasion, the prize was this new Universal oven. Although the elegantly attired winner may look a tad skeptical, surely her husband was thrilled.

REAL ESTATE AGENT. Standing next to her highway advertising sign is Cora, the wife of Bill Boosey. Her real estate office/antique store adjoined their 550-acre ranch where Boosey Road meets Highway 126. She was a businesswoman when few women claimed a career; he was a citrus rancher and a director on the Citizens State Bank Board. (Photograph courtesy of John Nichols Gallery.)

YOUR PRESENCE REQUESTED. The Glen City Theater's manager, Don Austin, lent his theater's opulent stage for the wedding of Lois Petrie and Henry Brogdon. As the couple had requested, all attendants and attendees wore Western garb, and the high school band provided musical serenades. The grand finale was when the newlyweds mounted their waiting steeds and galloped off down Main Street amid whistles and hoots from well-wishers.

Dick's Sandwich Shop, 1940s, Dick Richey (right)

DICK'S SANDWICH SHOP. Standing behind the counter are Gail Deaver and Dick Richey (right), ready to serve the locale clientele. Owned by Dick Dunbar, Dick's was notorious for having the best chili and beans. (Photograph courtesy of John Nichols Gallery.)

ROLLY'S PLACE. The owner of one of Main Street's popular eateries, Rolly Proebstel is caught here pouring a mug of coffee. Offering just one counter and some bar stools, he was notorious for having a cigarette dangling from his mouth while cooking. Consequently, it was not uncommon for a customer to find a sprinkling of telltale ashes on the plate of food.

Three

MAIN STREET
1950s

HOUSING DEVELOPMENT. Looking toward the southwest, at the old Nathan Blanchard homestead at the upper end of Palm Avenue, this image shows the roofs of the cookie-cutter-style houses of the first subdivision on the west end of town. Note the old drive-in movie screen between the trees. The Blanchard home, barn, gardens, and orchards were soon razed to make room for more housing. All that remains of the estate are a few of its stately conifers.

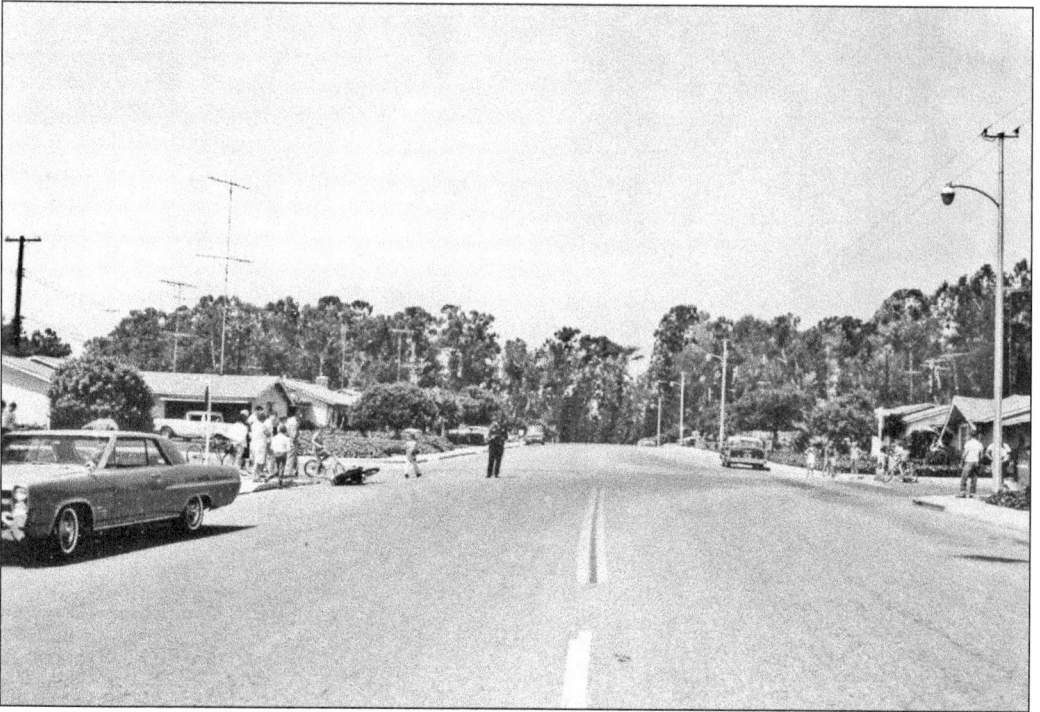

DOWNED MOTORCYCLE. Looking west on Santa Paula Street near its intersection with Bradley Street, the picture clearly shows a new subdivision in the style of the late 1950s. Following World War II, the city began to experience such housing developments on both the western and northern city limits. New families called for new schools: Glen City, Blanchard, and Bedell grammar schools were the answers. (Photograph courtesy of the Santa Paula Police Department.)

DEL KING SERVICE STATION, 1940. In recognition of the 50th anniversary of the founding of the Union Oil Company of California in Santa Paula, the 76 Station is tricked out in colorful flags and promotional banners. King managed the business for years. It was a "real" service station with Minute Men in crisp blue-and-white uniforms checking oil, washing windows, inspecting tire pressure, and filling the tank.

LEFFINGWELL CHEMICAL COMPANY. The buildings were used to warehouse the company's primary product, Foliar Nutrients. This was a blended fertilizer used to spray on citrus to enhance growth and productivity. The original use of the buildings was generating electricity for the Santa Paula Light Company, dating to 1896. Today it is Nutra-Chem and is located at 917 Railroad Avenue.

SANTA PAULA FEED AND SUPPLY. Lou Hengehold purchased the business in 1954. The building dates to 1888 when it warehoused sacks of lima beans and grains. He changed the name to the Mill, and so began the town's fond association with it and the Hengehold family. Lou, Polly, and seven children all worked here at some point. It is the new home of the Museum of Ventura County's farm implements.

JUE'S SUPERETTE, 233 HARVARD BOULEVARD. Opening in January 1958 with a gala celebration, the new grocery was owned by Jake Jue, a cofounder of the Ventura County Market. Jue was assisted by sons Willie, Harry, and Danny and daughters Jane and Helen; his wife, Mae Soo Hoo Jue, stayed home and managed their household. The market had the latest in modern machinery to keep meats, produce, and products fresh and offered beer and wine.

A CRIME SCENE? Fred H. Hall Radio and TV had been 16 years at this location, the corner of Eighth Street and Harvard Boulevard. His 1955 Christmas advertisement touted Motorola's television as being a viewer's dream because all tuning knobs were on the front of the set. The most expensive model on his showroom floor was the console for $369.95—an expensive luxury indeed. (Photograph courtesy of the Santa Paula Police Department.)

PRINDLE AUTO COURT. At the corner of Main and Eleventh Streets, it is obvious from his signage that Lee Prindle offered every kind of convenience to the touring public—from a fishing license to a room, a mini-market to a car wash shed. (Photograph courtesy of the Santa Paula Police Department.)

GLEN CITY THEATER BURNING, DECEMBER 1949. Opening in December 1919, this was a movie palace worthy of song, as the *Chronicle*'s editor warbled, "The initial note is sounded in the lobby where the grey walls are delicately frescoed with landscapes." The theater was an instant sensation. Forty years later, a December fire destroyed its opulent interior. The firefighters, shown here, could do nothing but prevent the flames from spreading—it was a total loss.

FOX WEST COAST THEATER PREMIER, OCTOBER 12, 1950. The *Santa Paula Chronicle* ran daily blurbs in anticipation of the grand opening, "All proceeds will benefit the Santa Paula Boys Club's new clubhouse project. The ultramodern theater to be the first in the county to have air conditioning. It has over 1000 seats, all with padded backs and self-rising seats for maximum comfort and viewing. There will be two separate glassed-in, sound proofed rooms for mothers with infants or young children. Bleachers to be built to accommodate the crowds. An array of Hollywood celebrities to attend the premier." A throng came and so did the movie stars. Among them were Eleanor Parker, Yvonne de Carlo, Jack Cronin, Rod Cameron, Forrest Tucker, and Chill Wills. *He's a Cock-Eyed Wonder* starring Mickey Rooney and Terry Moore was premiered. The theater was torn down in the mid-1960s.

CAUCH'S DRUGS. The name had been a Main Street staple since the 1880s. In 1946, Harold Ringle purchased the business but maintained the historic name. Through the years of Ringle's ownership, the store expanded and offered much more than just prescriptions. Shown here from left to right are Art Stopey and Walter Pendleton, both of whom were licensed pharmacists. (Photograph courtesy of John Nichols Gallery.)

CHAMBERS MARKET. Although the photograph dates from the 1950s, Russ Chambers acquired the firm in late 1938, having gained experience from operating a local wholesale produce business. He maintained the grocery side and leased out both the meat and liquor departments. It was housed in the old Balcom Hall building and burned under suspicious circumstances in the early 1960s.

SANTA PAULA MEMORIAL HOSPITAL. In the mid-1950s, the Thille family initiated the drive to build such a facility with a very substantial gift. Two other pioneer families, the Teagues and the McKevetts, donated the original land. Created to serve the entire Santa Clara River Valley, which included Fillmore and Piru, the Santa Paula Memorial Hospital received nearly $500,000 collectively donated by the valley residents. When completed, all contributors took pride in knowing their hospital was financed totally by their in-kind donations and monetary contributions.

AERIAL VIEW, SANTA PAULA AIRPORT. Opened in 1930 with the hangars seen closest to the freeway, the facility had experienced major expansion during the interim 25 years. Founded primarily by native son Ralph Dickenson and funded completely by local businessmen, the airport continues to be privately owned. Considered one of the busiest in the country, it also is known for its large collection of antique airplanes and for being the home of the Aviation Museum of Santa Paula.

Four

BEYOND MAIN STREET
AGRICULTURE AND OIL

A NATIVE AMERICAN LEGEND. The profile of the face of a Chumash maiden is identifiable atop South Mountain. Starting at the left side of the photograph, her throat, then chin and so forth, is seen with her long hair flowing away from her forehead. According to the myth, she saved her threatened village by throwing herself into the flooding waters of the Santa Clara River. Santa Paula is in the background, behind rows of verdant citrus orchards.

McDivitt Ranch, 1946. This photograph illustrates when citrus crops were in transition. The three blocks of young trees are lemons, which replaced old orange orchards. Interspersed are a few remaining mature oranges; in the far background are row crops. Because of the market demand for lemons—especially by the Japanese—oranges slipped as a viable cash crop. Today lands where orange orchards once thrived are also growing lemons, row crops, and nursery stock.

Teamwork. Into the 1950s, it was still possible to see individual farms or farming companies using horse or mule teams to work the fields. Even today, a few hearty souls or passionate traditionalists keep such animals just for the joy of driving a team or showing their grandchildren how things "used to be done."

MUPU ORANGE ASSOCIATION PACKINGHOUSE, 1944. Each packinghouse is owned, operated, and managed by a membership association of growers. Initially in the citrus business, oranges, both summer Valencias and winter navels, were the primary cash crop. In the spring, when trees were loaded with blossoms, the entire Santa Clara River Valley was a fragrant bouquet. Today just two of the original orange houses remain and both are vacant. There remains one operating lemon house.

LIMONEIRA PACKINGHOUSE. Mechanization had advanced the processes of citrus packing dramatically, and the appearance of uniforms indicates the company's interest in improving sanitary conditions. As the photograph shows, women still handled the sorting, sizing, and wrapping of each lemon in tissue-like paper. The heavy wooden field crates were the old standbys for hauling the fruit from the orchards; the lighter cardboard boxes on the conveyor belt were the new mode for shipping fruit.

LIMONEIRA RANCH FARM WORKER HOUSING, 1930S. Since citrus comes into production year-round, there was, and is, demand for a permanent workforce and permanent housing. Shown here is farmworker housing to help accommodate Limoneira's 1,500 employees. Each unit had electricity, hot and cold running water, baths, and toilets, with gas for cooking and heating. A minimal rental fee was charged to cover maintenance.

TENTING TONIGHT. Poisoning by gas was the alternative means to kill some citrus pests. Tent fumigation required coordination, caution, and the talents of four men. The work was done at night because of lower temperatures and less wind. Simply explained, the job required pulling a huge canvas tent over an orange tree that could be 20 feet high, securing it to the ground with a tight fit, and then "shooting" it inside with hydrocyanic acid gas. Tent fumigation ended in the 1950s.

WILLARD BECKLEY, 1930s. Fondly remembered as "Beck," Willard was well known and well respected by citrus growers throughout the Santa Clara River Valley and the Ojai. He had a degree in entomology, and during his 62-year career, he worked with the local Associates Insectary using biological controls and ended his long stint in the "bug" business by working for a local chemical pest control service. Here he poses by a hand-operated rig that smothered pests by spraying oil.

MORE MODERN SPRAY RIG. This all-in-one contraption allows the operator to stay inside the cab rather than standing on the platform and being exposed to the deadly fumes. It was more efficient in covering the trees because of the action of the oscillating boom, which applies an even coating of oil from a series of revolving and rocking guns on the central mast. Such machines are in use today.

CROP DUSTING, 1950s. The plane is a Stearman; the pilot is Ted Venegas. The biplane was the Army Air Corps' primary trainer for rookie pilots during World War II. After the war, it became the preferred craft by crop-dusting pilots because the double wings gave the plane more lift. Crop-dusting operators apply either pesticides or fertilizers on orchards and do so in early mornings or late afternoons. Ted Venegas was considered by many as the county's "Crop Dusting Ace." He piloted crop dusters for 45 years, 21 of which he operated out of his own business in the Santa Paula Airport. He owned both a Stearman and a Grumman Ag Cat, and when on the job, a waved hand from the ground received a friendly tip of the wing. Today only helicopters are used in Ventura County for better maneuverability.

HARRY REDDICK RANCH, 1955. Reddick was an engineer by education and profession and a rancher by vocation. In the 1940s, he introduced the idea of using contour planting for his hillside orchards to prevent erosion. His success prompted other growers to use the same technique, which led to more slopes being planted and increased agricultural acreage. Due to his contouring success, he was appointed the Regional Soil Conservation Service director. Here he is standing on top of the tractor (below) explaining to colleagues and farmers the advantages of the machinery called a "dam lister." Because of its unique design, when it is pulled on the contour of a hillside, rainfall is dammed and allowed to soak in. It was an invaluable alternative to the usual plowing up and down a hill, which led to rain run-off and disastrous soil erosion.

AN AWARD-WINNING ENTRY, 1950. Annually the staff of the County Agricultural Commissioner's office at one time created and assembled remarkable displays to promote local produce and boast the variety of crops Ventura County produced. The photograph preserves an award-winning exhibit at the state fair in Sacramento. In today's agricultural production standings, Ventura County ranks 10th in California—a noteworthy position considering over half of the county is protected forests or wildernesses.

A DRAMATIC CHANGE, TORREY FIELD. The apparatus in the foreground is called a jack line and dates to the 1890s. The partially seen steel derrick in the background is from the 1940s and may be seen today. The jack line was a unique development that allowed one 25-horsepower engine to pump many wells by using an eccentric wheel and cables attached to each wellhead. Torrey was one of Union Oil's oldest producing fields.

DRILLING AND PUMPING. The far derrick is rigged for drilling. The in-between five beam pumping units are in place because there is insufficient natural gas to push the crude to the service. The rig in the foreground has a pumping unit over its well—unusual because the derrick was generally removed if the well proved out and was then replaced with a pumping device.

OAK RIDGE OIL COMPANY COMMUNITY POSTCARD. The company's South Mountain Field dates to the early 1920s. So extensive was the operation that a small development was built, providing offices, storage facilities, dormitory-style living quarters, a dining hall, and so forth. Drilling took place 24 hours a day, seven days a week, and at night lights from the derricks were seen for miles. Texaco took over the company in the 1930s. (Photograph courtesy of John Nichols Gallery.)

Texaco Crew, 1940s. This is a photograph of one-half of the oil field force that worked in the South Mountain Field.

Men of Oil Patch, 1930s. The jaunty gents are a well pulling crew, which meant they came onto the rig when a change in equipment needed to be made in the hole of a well, like changing a bit. Posing from left to right are Argyle Stewart, Othal Autry, Raymond Daries, and Lloyd Barmore.

Five

OUR TOWN'S PEOPLE

KOTO AND YASUO CHIDA FAMILY, 1932. Yasuo Chida emigrated from Japan in 1907 and came to Santa Paula in 1914. Hired by the Teague-McKevett Ranch to work in the lemon packinghouse, he was the first Japanese to be employed there and was instrumental in getting the company to hire more of his countrymen. From left to right are Tokio, mother Koto, Sachiko, father Yasuo, and Takeshi.

JAUREGUI FAMILY. Above, from left to right are Daniel Robert, Andrew, Peter, Gracion, Anthony, and Edward with mother, Isabel, and father, Frank. Antonio Jauregui came first to California as a Basque sheepherder in the mid-1800s. Frank was one of his sons and continued the tradition. With his Basque wife, Isabel, they bought the ranch in Wheeler Canyon in 1905. There they raised their 13 children and ran herds of sheep and cattle in the foothills. Below, from left to right are (first row) Isabel, Frank, Catherine Belle, Francis, and Marie; (second row) Annie, Lillian, and Grace; not pictured is Josephine. Understandably, it was difficult to get the whole family together. The exception was when Isabel had a stroke and died. Everyone was home within hours.

PIONEER DESCENDANTS.
George Washington
Faulkner arrived in 1876
and purchased his ranch
west of town. His wife's
name was Rhoda, and they
had two daughters, Stella
and Alpha. Alpha married
Farel Ayers. This is a
photograph of the Ayers
family in 1936. Posing
from left to right are Farel,
Alpha, Loren, Raymond,
Rhoda, and Stella.

LETHA BRIDGES AND
DAUGHTERS. A young
widow, Bridges managed to
raise her girls by working
at Blumenthal's, one
of Main Street's finest
department stores. Lined
up according to age, the
girls from left to right
are Beatrice, Marjorie,
Annis, and Mary, whose
hair her mother, Letha,
is fixing for the camera.

49

BLANCHE AND MANNING ROGERS FAMILY. From left to right are Blanche holding Nancy and Manning with son Roland. The occasion was the baptism of the baby. Blanche Rogers was a longtime elementary school teacher.

THE FLYING DICKENSONS. John Marshall Dickenson married Ida Belle Hawley, came to Santa Paula, and bought his ranch west of town, all in 1886. He raised walnuts, and they raised four children, two of whom are shown here. Ralph stands next to his mother, with brother Marshall at his side. Both sons were pilots and had their own planes. Ralph was influential in developing the Santa Paula Airport.

NINE FINE NAVARRO
DAUGHTERS. From left
to right are (first row)
Rebecca, father Rafael,
mother Esther, and Rosa;
(second row) Esther, Jovita,
Frances, Hope, Virginia,
Elvira, and Mary.

AN EXTENDED FAMILY GATHERING, MOTHER'S DAY, 1938. From left to right are (first row) Ruth
Avendaño, Cecilio, Angela, and Estella Preciado, Helen Jimenez, Viola Preciado, Sam Avendaño,
and Zeke Sanchez; (second row) Cecilio Huerta, Ruben Preciado, Virginia Huerta, Mary, Rosa,
and Esther Preciado, Esther and Jose Preciado, Esther Huerta, Manuel and Mercedes Aviña;
Andrea Preciado Sanchez; Cesario Huerta; and Jesus Jimenez holding Ray Jimenez; (third row)
Beatrice and Julia Huerta and Joe and Leon Preciado.

TRUE PIONEER STOCK. Norman Richardson's grandfather George Richardson was the original homesteader in 1867. Norman continued to run stock on the property as well as plant various tree crops. Norman married Ida Smith, a schoolmate and sister of Lucy Smith, who married Douglas Shively; the sisters' name combination gave Santa Paula Lucada Street, which marks the location of the Smith ranch. Posing here from left to right are Norman, Norma, Virginia, Ida, and son Roger.

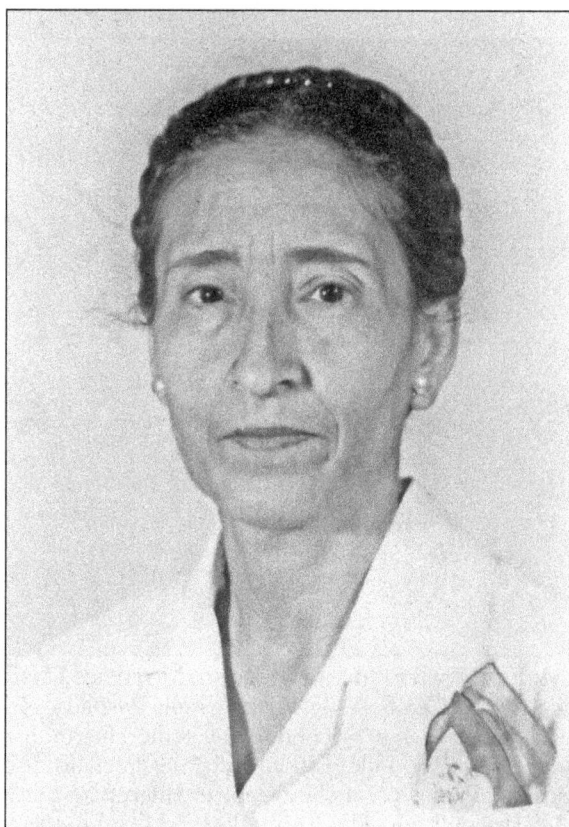

CARMEN DE LEON. Born in Mexico and the eldest of 11 children, Carmen's parents came to the area in 1914. As a youngster, she pitted apricots and developed her own technique that was so fast none could beat her. She was known as "Queen of the Apricots." Never marrying, in later years she adopted her young nephew Xavier Montes. Theirs was an abiding bond that lasted until her passing.

A YOUNG FAMILY. Amada and Augustine Reyes pose behind their children, David and Rose. She was a seasonal employee at a chili factory in Oxnard and he was a union laborer. Rose excelled in her studies, graduated from the high school with honors, and attained a college education.

A SUCCESSFUL GARDENER. Manuel Gonzales was a well-known gardener about town and had a growing business before his untimely death. The tragedy required his wife, Helen (née Soto), to work various occupations in order to raise the children. She too was successful. Shown here are, from left to right, (first row) Robert, Helen, Richard, and Vela; (second row) Manuel.

THREE GENERATIONS. From left to right are (first row) unidentified, Alan Teague, Judy Teague, Kathleen Cox, and Winifred Cox; (seated) Maiya Teague, Milton Teague, Harriet McKevett Teague, Charles Collins Teague, Alice Teague Cox, Charles Teague, and unidentified; (third row) Alfrida Poco Teague, John Cox, and two unidentified individuals.

OLD-TIME FAMILIES. George Harding was a businessman, a skilled horseman, and instrumental in organizing both the Santa Paula Rodeo and the Boys Club. Mildred King Harding was a third-generation Santa Paulan as the daughter of Warren King, of King Furniture fame, who was the son of the town's pioneer photographer, C. E. King. She was an excellent pianist and a welcomed performer at many social gatherings.

A FORMAL PORTRAIT. Posing are Lai King Wong and her husband, Herbert Jung. Even though he was the youngest brother of Joe and Jake Jue, the immigration authorities on his passport misspelled his name. (When alone and 16, it is best not argue about spelling.) With his brother Joe's sons, John and Donald, he ran the farm in Santa Paula. Later another was bought in Oxnard, which also provided fresh produce for the family's markets.

CHILDHOOD SWEETHEARTS. Pictured are Lucy (née Smith) and Douglas Shively. She studied to be a concert pianist, and he became the president of the Citizens State Bank. She also became quite an organist; he also became quite an artist.

FIRST LIBRARIAN. Sarah Blanchard was the daughter of Ann Elizabeth and Nathan Blanchard, the "Father of Santa Paula." Since her parents were the donors of the Dean Hobbs Blanchard Memorial Library and as she believed education and books were paramount to success, "Miss Sarah" served as the librarian for years. Her tenure set the tone for future library boards to hire only licensed, well-qualified librarians.

JOE NESBITT. A college-educated cowboy from Arizona, he served in both World War II and Korea and came to Santa Paula in 1942 with his wife, Louise (née Grafe). He was a member of the Rancheros Visitadores and a true cattleman; being a banker had never been a consideration. However, circumstances led to his becoming president of the Citizens State Bank in 1978, a position he held competently for many years.

GRAFE CALLAHAN CONSTRUCTION COMPANY. Paul Grafe's company was a national operation, which specialized in major projects such as dams, canals, and bridges. In the 1940s, he purchased for his family's home the beautiful Ferndale Ranch, which had been the E. L. Doheny's summer retreat. Paul and Helen Grafe are shown here with their daughter Louise Grafe Nesbitt, who sometime later changed her name to "Sally Lou."

HIS HONOR. Edwin "Ed" Beach discovered Santa Paula as a gymnast when his Pasadena City College team competed with the high school. He was impressed by coach Randall Bryden, the small community, and the tree-lined streets. After a three-year stint in the army and earning his law degree, he and his wife, Janet, moved here. His career advanced from a private practice to an associate justice of the state appellate court, from which he retired in 1986.

A PARTNERSHIP BUILT. Barringer and Botke was a well-known contracting firm during the 1960s. Bill Botke was the son of artists Jesse Arms and Cornelis Botke. Initially, there were two Barringers, brothers John and Carl. Coming in 1947, when architect Roy Wilson Sr. suggested a possible job here, their bid won and all stayed. John's moving prompted the name change. Shown are the partners, Bill (front left) sitting catty-corner from wife Kay and Carl sitting catty-corner from wife Cathy.

EL CHARRO. Mateo Marquez is wearing the regional costume of his native Jalisco, Mexico. He is dressed for a Fiesta Parade in which he always rode his magnificent white Arabian. Marquez was the founder of Marquez Bakery, which for years was a popular business. His son David successfully assumed management following his retirement.

VENTURA BEAUTY SCHOOL'S GRADUATION. These gowned graduates stand behind their models, who are modeling specially created hairdos. The second row includes, from left to right, Florence Elwell, Virginia Ariza, Lucy Contreras, Clara Coronado, and an unidentified individual. Seated on the left is Florence Valdes, and the rest are unidentified. Florence quit hair curling, took up Mexican cooking, and opened Tia Babes Burritos. For over 30 years, the popular business has satisfied generations of happy customers.

AN EARLY ANESTHESIOLOGIST. Dr. Ralph Busch came to the area at the behest of Dr. Artemas Strong in 1961 to help him develop and head the anesthesiology department for the new Santa Paula Hospital. As such, Dr. Busch was the second county specialist in that particular field. From left to right are (first row) Ralph B. Busch III ("Trey"), Jeffrey, and Gregory; (second row) father Ralph holding twin Ellyn ("Lyn"), mother Deedee holding twin Frank ("Paco"), and Peter.

ONE OF THE NEW DOCTORS. The young Carlson family came to town in 1950 after Dr. Ernie Carlson finished his residency at the county hospital. They then lived briefly in North Carolina, where he served as an Indian reservation physician. Upon returning, in addition to his practice, he assumed a leading role in founding the Santa Paula Memorial Hospital. From left to right are mother Joyce, Susan, father Ernie holding Carol, Mark, Paul, and David.

REV. TOM BOUSEMAN AND FAMILY. Dr. Bouseman was the Presbyterian minister for many years. His parents were missionaries in the Philippines when World War II began; Tom was just a boy. Captured by the Japanese, they and hundreds of other civilians were held in a horrible detention camp for the duration. From left to right are (first row) Rick, Rob, and Kathy; (second row) Peggy, father Tom, and mother Ellie.

LAST STATION AGENT. John Woodworth, his wife, Theda, and son John Jr. came to Santa Paula in 1954. An employee of the Southern Pacific, Woodworth was a resident agent; he needed to be at the depot all the time, so he and the family lived upstairs in the old wooden station, which dated to 1887. Their living quarters amounted to a four-room apartment that came with all the amenities, including an office where he conducted his business.

THE GOOD DOCTOR AND FAMILY. Dr. Artemas Strong, a native son whose father, Jacob, was also a local physician, completed his medical education and returned home to practice. Louise Harpham Strong had led an exciting life prior to marriage as a student of the arts, a European traveler, and a seeker of knowledge, qualities she and her husband shared and interests they pursued together. From left to right are Camilla, father Artemas, mother Louise, and Bill.

BLAINE ROMNEY. Romney received his law degree from George Washington University. His credentials aided in getting government employment during the Depression. Joining the air force, he served in various positions as an adjutant and was discharged as a major. Blaine married Jeanette Hardison, and in 1946 they came home to her hometown. The counselor was appointed Santa Paula's city attorney that same year—a position he held for many years.

MAKING SAND CASTLES. Dana Teague, portrait photographer extraordinaire, was the source of the professionally taken family photographs included in this book. With his wife, Ruth, his most able and entertaining assistant, they were always able to make anyone photogenic. The photographer is unidentified, but he or she must have had held up a funny birdie. From left to right are Suzanne, father Dana holding Timothy, mother Ruth (née Reddick), and Dana B. Teague.

THE COUNSELOR BEACH AND FAMILY. Posing in their garden, on a huge boulder from nearby Santa Paula Creek, from left to right are (seated) John, Janet, Carol, Jeanne, and David; (standing) Tom and Ed. Still to come were daughters Anne and Meg.

63

THE WILDE BUNCH.
Irv Wilde's degree as a hydraulic engineer served him and the United Water District well. His wife, Delphine (née Joy), was a longtime and popular Briggs School teacher. From left to right are (first row) Alice Eiline, grandfather Ray C. Joy, and Patricia Delphine; (second row) Christine Ellen, Joy Ernestine, Mary Kathline, Delphine Joy, Roger, and George Irvin "Irv."

THREE MORE GENERATIONS OF PIONEER FAMILIES. From left to right are (first row) Gordon Eugene Kimball, Ann Louise Kimball, and Margaret Jean Kimball; (second row) John Kelly Thille holding Nicholas Matthew Thille, Dorcas Anne Hardison Kimball Thille holding Peter Timothy Thille, R. Logan Hardison holding Jeanine Louise Hardison, Carol Essert Hardison holding Michael Logan Hardison, and Thomas Allen Hardison; (third row) Bob and Mary Louise Hardison.

Six

"I Do!"

THE ROMERO WEDDING. Many Santa Paula couples grew up together, went to school together, and married each other. Here family and friends gathered to share in the special occasion with Rebecca (née Navarro) and Carlos Romero.

STUNNING IN SATIN. Depicted is Francisca and Fidel Corona's wedding party.

HE FELL FOR A FILLMORE LADY. Native son Max Rudolph and Gwen Hart were married in Fillmore in June 1936. Max's high school English teacher, Helen Hardison, played Cupid by introducing them. They spent their honeymoon at the old Miramar Hotel in Montecito.

A MEMORABLE OCCASION. A family celebrates the marriage of their children, Selma and Boyd. From left to right are Thomas Clyde Strange, Emma Desolee Strange, groom Boyd Linton, bride Selma Katherine, Lissie Ethel Foster, and Benjamin Foster.

A HAPPY COUPLE. The wedding day of Geneva Stewart and Loren Ayers is depicted here. The very short minister stood on a step between the very tall bride and groom.

A JAUREGUI SON IS MARRIED. Theresa Gaiardo and Joe Jauregui were married in Camarillo's St. Mary Magdalene Catholic Church. They met at a dance in Saticoy. Theresa's parents were Italian immigrants who settled in the Santa Rosa Valley on their walnut ranch. She was an avid student and taught her mother how to read using comic books. Joe was in the sheep business with brothers Gracion and Robert in Wheeler Canyon as the Jauregui Brothers.

GARDEN WEDDING PARTY. Standing on the far right are the newlyweds, Ray Holts and his bride, Frances (née Greenough). Joining them from left to right are (gentlemen) J. Frank Greenough (Frances's father) and Howard McDonald; (ladies) Marada McDonald and Mabel Greenough (Frances's mother).

A FORMAL WEDDING, FIRST PRESBYTERIAN CHURCH. Posing are, from left to right, (seated) ring bearer Zeke Preciado Sanchez and flower girl Helen Preciado Jimenez; (standing) bridesmaid Mary Louise Tirre, usher Isabel ("Chito") Prieto, bridesmaid Saca Sonora, usher Robert Bustamante, maid of honor Esther Huerta Preciado, groom John Ruiz, bride Rosa Huerta Preciado, best man Manuel Estrada, bridesmaid Julia Huerta, usher Lee Coronado, bridesmaid Linda Prieto, and usher Raymond Rosales.

AN ELEGANT WEDDING RECEPTION. The newlyweds, Kathleen (née Cox) and Harold Hobson, are in the home of her parents, Alice and John Cox. Her smiling sister Winifred looks on.

CAROL JEAN BROWN MARRIED A PHYSICIAN.
Carol Jean and Dr. John "Jack" Shilton
were married in 1947 and spent their
honeymoon motoring across Canada to
visit his family in Chicago and returned via
the southern route. They traveled in a 1946
Chevrolet gunmetal-grey convertible with
red leather seats. It was Carol Jean's college
graduation and 21st birthday gift and one
of the first cars built after World War II.

THE CITY GIRL AND THE COWBOY.
Joanne and Richard Cummings's
wedding reception was held at the
California Club in Los Angeles.
Having known little of country
life, her moving to a small house
on his Wheeler Canyon ranch
was "the biggest jump in my life.
Friends were actually betting that
I wouldn't make it!" Their 50th
anniversary proved them wrong.

ANTONIO DIAZ TAKES A BRIDE. His marriage to Celia Leon ensured the continuation of his family's restaurant, Las Quinces Letras. With them as a team and then with their children, the popular place is now Familia Diaz and continues to be a favorite local institution.

THE BRIDE, HER SISTERS, AND PARENTS. Posing with their mother and father, Mattie and Clark Richards, are seven lovely daughters. The attendants were dressed in coral or aqua gowns. From left to right are (first row) Theresa, Cynthia, Roberta, Marcela, and Claudia; (second row) Eleanor, bride Carolyn, and Mattie and Clark Richards.

RUTH REYES WEDS FIDEL PEREZ. The maid of honor, Delfina Perez, is wearing peacock blue. The best man is Raymond Hernandez. The bridesmaids are wearing shocking pink and are (order unknown) Dolores Cervantes, Socorro Martinez, Carol Pina, Beatrice Garcia, Becky Gaeta, and Stella Qunitero. The ushers are (order unknown) Rudy Fuerte, Mike Ziegler, Max Vasquez, Sammy Reyes, Fred Osuna, and Norbet Riesgo. The flower girls are Cheryl Pacheco and Debra Hernandez; the ring bearer, Raymond Carrillo.

FIFTIETH WEDDING ANNIVERSARY. The happy celebrants, Mabel and J. Frank Greenough, are joined by, from left to right, Terry Holts, Frances Holts holding her granddaughter Lynda, Phil Holts, and Ray Holts.

Seven

LEARNING AND LEADING

McKevett School, 1932. Tokio Chida stands in the front on the right. Originally called North Grammar School, the school name was changed to recognize the pioneering family who gifted the property in 1926. The grades served were kindergarten through sixth grade. Students went on to Isbell Junior High (Middle) School. There was another elementary school on the south side of town called South Grammar School.

BARBARA WEBSTER SCHOOL PHOTOGRAPH, EIGHTH GRADE, 1939. From left to right are (first row) teacher Ida Mason (from Lawrence, Kansas) and Joe Rosas; (second row) Benny Arellano, Lupe Frescas, John Hernandez, Phillip Villarreal, Ruben Preciado, Noah ?, Alfredo Soto, Miguel Viramontes, and Max Vasquez; (third row) unknown, Mike Alvarez, Joe Velador, John Velador, Arthur Hernandez, Tony de Anda, Eugene Vaca, Crispin Vaca, and Miguel Diaz; (fourth row) ? Salvadez, Ernest Barboa, Jesus Torres, John Hernandez, Natividad Garcia, Mike Guerrero, Pablo Herrera, Salvador Sanchez, and Frank Molina.

ISBELL SCHOOL, EIGHTH GRADE, MAY 1936. From left to right are (first row) Joe Dunbar, Virginia Taft, Frances Turney, unidentified, Dorothy Borgeson, Dorothy Lefevre, Carmen ?, Sachiko Chida, Alahondra Nava, two unidentified, and Bill Jones; (second row) unidentified, Dick Kline, Barbara Foster, unidentified, June Webster, Hildred Hawkins, Frances Hardison, teacher Charlotte Yarborough, Helen Webb, Barbara Meyer, Bobby Allen, Robert Procter, and Principal ? Coeker; (third row) Robert Shaw, Harold Bartley, Madison Caldwell, Billy Edde, Jimmy Yarborough, George Bond, Ventura County Schools superintendant, William Colburn, Barry Baumgartner, Vernon Mashburn, Clarence Eastburn, and Louis Meyer.

BARBARA WEBSTER SCHOOL CLASS PHOTOGRAPH, EIGHTH GRADE, 1942 OR 1943. The smiling lady on the right is principal Barbara Webster, for whom the school was renamed from Canyon School. It hosted kindergarten through eighth grade, and then all students went into the high school.

HOME ECONOMICS PROJECT. The 1950s were the years of layers of petticoats, the more voluminous the better. All Isbell eighth-grade girls were required to make full skirts to show off their starched crinolines. This photograph shows the young author of this book, Mary Alice Orcutt, standing behind her good friend Louise Freedle while awkwardly attempting to make "devil horns" over her head.

A Favorite Physical Education Teacher.
Elizabeth Ramsey taught girls physical
education at Isbell for years. A natural
athlete as well mentor and friend of her
students, Ramsey remained active with
young women even after retirement by being
involved on an administrative level with
the Tres Condados Girl Scout Council.

The New Santa Paula Union High School Campus, 1939. Built with Public Works
Administration (PWA) financing, the project took nearly three years to complete. Reflecting
the popular Spanish-Mediterranean style, the most striking feature remains the blue-tiled bell
tower. Equally striking is the Freeman Eakin Memorial Auditorium with its distinctive artwork
specially created for the building. The most outstanding is the mural in the foyer designed and
painted by Jesse Arms and Cornelis Botke.

THE PRINCIPLED PRINCIPAL. Freeman Eakin served as the high school principal/superintendent for 25 years, during which his devotion to the students, affection for his community, and unabashed enthusiasm for all school sports were legendary. Every yearbook carried his personal inspiration to the graduates. An example stated, "May these pages always be a challenge to you to accomplish, to become, to do, and to be yourself at any cost."

GIRLS HOCKEY TEAM, 1935. From left to right are (kneeling) captain Rosie Huerta Preciado, Nellie Mahan, Virginia ?, Mertal Rithul, Mildred Ammumia, Martha Hoffmiester, and Coach Wilson; (standing) Virginia Cline, Helen Jean Shipley, Beverly Russell, Iris Griffin, Rosie Fernandez, Emma Dare, Mary McCall, and Dolores Sanchez.

BIG MAN ON CAMPUS. Roger Boles lettered in all sports, was both captain of the football team and quarterback in his senior year, and served as student body president. He received an engineering degree from the University of Southern California in 1934. In recognition of his achievements in school and in the military, his family established the Roger Boles Award, awarded annually to the most outstanding boy in the senior class.

EL SALANO STAFF
B. Sharp, Warren, Shipley, Teague,
A. Sharp, Eakin, Cline, Wilson.

AWARD WINNING EL SOLANO STAFF, 1935. The diligence and dedication of these students were the determining factors for their yearbook's national honor. The yearly All-American Competition rating score gave the high school's annual 865 points out of a possible 1,000. Areas of consideration were financial status, mechanical aspects, editing, plan, and theme.

BOMBS AWAY! Footballer Jess Victoria launches into a flying leap in his attack on a tackle bag.

A 1937 GRADUATE. Rachel Huerta Avendano graduated from Santa Paula High in 1937.

WARTIME PICKERS, 1942. Due to the labor shortage caused by drafted agricultural workers, the high school went on a half-day schedule so students could help. Here the smiling coeds show off their lemon harvest. From left to right are (seated) unidentified, Modene Reed, Barbara Kerslake, Norma Trombley, Betty Guinn, and Peggy Pusey; (kneeling) Pat Freeman; (standing) Bessie Furr, Frieda Welch, Carol Jean Brown, Betty Smith, Virginia Gunderson, Madge Bradley, and Betty Lee Perkins. (Photograph courtesy of *El Solano*.)

SCRAP COLLECTORS. While the girls toiled in the orchards, the boys did whatever else needed doing to help the farmers. They smudged, drove tractors, irrigated, hoed weeds, and helped with the harvests. The student body collected tons of scrap metal and purchased hundreds of dollars worth of war bonds. Joe Mashburn stands on the heap. (Photograph courtesy of *El Solano*.)

SPORTSWOMEN, CLASS OF 1949. Girls' Athletic Association members in their letter sweaters are, from left to right, (seated) Shirley Crusey, Beverly Been, Mary Vasay, France Reyes, Rachel Villa, Marcell Hepworth, Pat McConnell, Isabel A. Coverrobias, Ofelia Urias, and Barbara Jean Felderbaum; (standing) Alice Dominguez, Imogene Morris, Dorothy Condrew, unidentified, Nana Gardner, Barbra Bennett, Ann Cline, Janet Watson, Sarah Leavens, Jean Cash, Angela Huerta Preciado, and Barbara Butler.

A REAL BALANCING ACT, 1941. The school's gymnastics team excelled under the guidance and inspiration of coach Randall Bryden. An exceptional gymnast himself, in 1933 he held the world record in the rope climb. He came to the high school in 1937 where he enjoyed a long and successful career. The year of this photograph, his team won the first of what would be many California Interscholastic Federation Championship honors. (Photograph courtesy of *El Solano*.)

THE AMERICAN FIELD SERVICE (AFS).
The AFS was organized in 1947 as an
international exchange of students
who would live with foreign families
and hopefully break down cultural
and geographical barriers. The high
school's first student came in 1952; the
program became an important part of
the curriculum and the community for
years. This photograph shows 1953's
student, Klaus Ulbricht from Germany,
who is standing between Glen Gessford
(left) and Phil Holts. Seated are Irene
Ayala (left) and Marilyn Kelsey. The four
high school juniors spent the coming
summer abroad as part of the program.

RHE NELSON AND KLAUS ULBRICHT. Rhe came to the school in the 1930s as a history teacher
and was the primary force behind its involvement in the AFS program. She dedicated her life to
teaching history and promoting world friendship and goodwill. Throughout her long career, she
befriended both hundreds of her students and those who came from foreign lands.

ROUND-UP. It remains a year-end tradition of fun, games, and silliness. "Sittin' a spell" is zany Bill Orcutt and his not-so-corny pal and exchange student Klaus Ulbricht.

PROUD GRADUATES. On the left is Helen Jue with her good friend Irene Alvarez.

LOCAL JOCKS. After graduation, some men joined sports teams, one of those sponsored by local businesses. The competition was stiff, the games were well publicized in the *Chronicle*, and no doubt, the fans were raucous. Dick's Team referred to Dick Dunbar, who owned the Santa Paula Bakery and Sandwich Shop. In the first row, from left to right, are Roger Munger, unidentified, Johnny Burleson, and unidentified. In the second row, third from left, is Richard Dunbar.

A SPECIAL EVENT, 1935. The 20-30 Club was Santa Paula's newest fraternal organization. The occasion was president Del King's receiving the official charter from the district governor. Some 160 district members and their wives shared in the celebration. It was a popular national association founded by young men who felt service clubs were dominated and run by older men who only elected their peers as officers.

ALIANZA HISPANO-AMERICANA SOCIETY, 1937. This fraternal benefit society founded in 1894 offered membership for Mexican Americans. At a time when citizens could not depend upon government-sponsored social programs or labor unions, the alliance provided low-cost life insurance as well as cultural and social activities. For this photograph, the members and their families gather in the Casa Del Mexicano.

SANTA PAULA'S REBEKAH LODGE. Unfortunately, the names are unknown, but the occasion is the installation of new members. The Rebekah Degree is an honorary one, conferred upon wives and daughters of members of the International Order of Odd Fellows (IOOF). They share the same goal as their Odd Fellow brothers: "To improve and elevate the character of mankind" by abiding by their basic tenets of friendship, love, and truth.

CASA DEL MEXICANO, C. 1940. Established in Los Angeles in 1931, this continues to be a popular membership organization catering to the Hispanic communities through cultural, social, and civic activities as well as helping members in need. The founding members pictured here are, from left to right, (first row) Juan Ruiz, unidentified, Andrea Mendoza, Al Pienada, Juan Salas, Jose Diaz, and four unidentified individuals; (second row) Lorenzo Aviña, Toni Salas, Estella Salas, Juana Marquez, Carmen Argüelles, three unidentified, Josefa Diaz, and four unidentified individuals; (third row) Ysmael Gonzales, Maxine Gonzales, Maria Aviña, eight unidentified, Nomie Salas, Virginia Marquez, Estella Escobedo, Conception Salas, and Tommie Solis; (fourth row) unidentified, ? Mora, ? Cuervas, and six unidentified individuals.

YOUTH GROUP, 1941. This group was organized and led by Rev. Luis Tirre of the Spanish Community Missionary Church (*El Buen Pastor*). From left to right are (first row) Anita Barajas, unidentified, Frances Escarsega, Carrie Sonora, Eleanor Cisneros, unidentified, Paz Marquez, Virginia Escarsega, Mary Louise Tirre, Estella Colmenares, and Toni Salas; (second row) two unidentified, Conchito Delgado, Maria Tirre, Sara Cisneros, Estella Salas, and Luoy Escarsega; (third row) Elaine Cisneros, Pastor Tirre, and Ruben Huerta Preciado.

SANTA PAULA LITTLE LEAGUE, 1957. Proudly posing is the first All-Star team of the new league, the first to receive the Little League charter. The field is still at the Boys and Girls Club. From left to right are (first row) Charles Lovio, Bruce Puckett, Roger Pendleton, and Mike Lamont; (second row) Don Buettner, Ed Mendoza, Sam Echavarria, Roy Coy, Paul Rudolph, Rick Ramsey, and manager William Stinnett; (third row) Joe Samples, Xavier Arellano, Tom Harris, David Inglis, Joe Jauregui, and Jim Colburn (who played in the major leagues).

Eight

OUR HEROES

RAY AYERS (LEFT) AND PAUL LATSKE, C. 1932. The two Santa Paula friends joined the National Guard and were stationed in Long Beach. They signed up to be assured of getting a free meal three times a week at the unit's headquarters. It was the Depression, money was scarce, and they had big appetites.

CESARIO HUERTA II, WORLD WAR II.
This seaman 2nd-class gunner was
stationed on the carrier *Enterprise*.
During air raids, he was in the turrets to
photograph the attacking enemy planes.

JOSEPH HUERTA AVENDANO, WORLD WAR II.
Enlisting in the air force, with his squadron in
England, he made many raids over the continent.
His participation in the bombing of Rumanian oil
fields brought him the Distinguished Flying Medal
and 17 Oak Leaf Clusters. Captain Avendano flew
over 22 missions and was killed just before going
home. He stands here with his older brother, Daniel.

THE FIVE MORENO BROTHERS, WORLD WAR II. Shown in this painting from left to right are Isaiah, private 1st class, army; Walter, captain, air force; Danny, special sergeant, Army Air Corps, in Germany; Abraham, private 1st class, army, in England; and Sammy, private 1st class, Army Air Force, in Japan.

DONALD JUE, WORLD WAR II. Having driven the family's grocery delivery vehicle, in boot camp he was assigned to the motor pool. Stationed in the Philippines, after its liberation he was an ambulance driver. Later, because of his grocery training, he managed the post's grocery store and at the time of his discharge was being trained to drive a tank with the rank of technician sergeant.

JOE GALLADOS JR., WORLD WAR II. On furlough from the army, he poses here with his mother, Rosa, and grandmother Esther Navarro.

RAMON AND ISABEL PRIETO, WORLD WAR II. Isabel joined the marines and was shipped out to the Pacific theater. Private 1st Class Prieto was killed in Bougainville during a night raid. His brother Ramon, on the left, was a private 1st class in the army. He was among the paratroopers dropped behind the enemy lines during Operation Overlord when killed.

HARVEY BROTHERS, DECORATED PILOTS, WORLD WAR II. On the left is Wayne; two years younger than Roger, he was an Army Air Corps pilot with the 400th Bomb Group and served in the South Pacific theater, where he completed 50 missions for which he was awarded the Distinguished Flying Cross and the Air Medal. Roger was also an Army Air Corps pilot but with the 398th Bomb Group. He served in the European theater and completed 32 missions over Germany and occupied countries. He was awarded the Distinguished Flying Cross, the Air Medal, and three Oak Leaf Clusters. The brothers were the sons of Mattie and Mac Harvey and were raised on the property known as Arroyo del Oso Rancho in the upper Ojai.

ROGER BOLES, WORLD WAR II. He served with Admiral Halsey's 3rd Fleet in the Philippines. As commander of a fighter squadron off the carrier *Lexington*, he led successful raids on Japanese installations. The day before he was to go home, he was shot down leading a strafing attack on the Lipa airfield. Posthumously he was awarded the Distinguished Flying Cross and a Gold Star.

MANUEL VICTORIA, WORLD WAR II. He and his three brothers, Joe, Manuel, and Jess, enlisted shortly after Pearl Harbor. Manuel was an army technical sergeant in Italy.

JESS VICTORIA, WORLD WAR II. He was a corporal in the Infantry Medic with the 123rd Regiment in the Pacific theater. He received the Bronze Star for running through enemy fire to save a downed soldier.

JOE VICTORIA, WORLD WAR II. A corporal in the Army Air Corps, Joe Victoria was sent to the Philippines. He was captured by the Japanese and spent 40 months in a prison camp; when released, he weighed 98 pounds. Reenlisting, he was discharged in 1948 as a sergeant.

RODOLFO "RUDY" VICTORIA, COAST GUARD, WORLD WAR II. When he asked his mother which branch he should join, she stated the Coast Guard was the best, "You won't get shot or have to kill anyone."

LEON HUERTA PRECIADO, WORLD WAR II.
Army private 1st class, Leon was in the 951st
Field Artilleries Battalion, European theater,
and with the 8th Corps Artillery, which fought
from Utah Beach to the Elbe River. Later in the
Korean Conflict, he made master sergeant.

**RUBEN HUERTA
PRECIADO, WORLD
WAR II.** Leon's
brother, Ruben
was a corporal
in the Army Air
Corps in the
Pacific theater.

MARY LOUISE TIRRE AND FRANK VARGAS, WORLD WAR II. Army Private 1st Class Vargas first served as a military police escort for German prisoners in Pennsylvania. Next he was deployed to the Papua Islands and New Guinea campaigns, for which he received five Overseas Service Bars, an Asiatic Pacific Campaign Ribbon, two Bronze Stars, and a Good Conduct Medal. While he was in the service, his wife, Mary Louise, worked and was a volunteer in the Santa Paula Civil Defense.

PEDRO DOMINGUEZ, WORLD WAR II. Dominguez served in the army, where he was a prisoner of war in Germany for two years. He reenlisted for the Korean Conflict.

97

PETE ROMERO, WORLD WAR II. Romero served in the Asiatic-Pacific campaign as a staff sergeant in the 145th Infantry Regiment of the 37th Division and was also a squad leader. He was awarded the Philippines Liberation Ribbon, Bronze Star, two Purple Hearts, Good Conduct, and World War II Victory Medal.

RICHARD CUMMINGS, WORLD WAR II. Joining the air force, Lieutenant Cummings stands here between two friends at Luke Air Force Base, Arizona. Though trained to be a fighter pilot, he was selected to be a flight instructor. His training plane was the AT-6 Texan, which was the aerial classroom for the majority of the Allied pilots who flew in World War II. Called a pilot's airplane, it could roll, loop, spin, snap, and vertical roll.

RICHARD VILLA, WORLD WAR
II. Instead of becoming a fighter
pilot, because he was bilingual,
Lieutenant Villa was assigned as a
flying instructor in the lend-lease
program, providing materials and
assistance to the Allied countries
in Central and South America and
Mexico. After his brother Herman
was killed in the Korean Conflict,
the lieutenant reenlisted and flew
over 270 combat missions over there.

ROBERT BUSTAMANTE, WORLD WAR
II. He was an electronics technician
4th-grade in the Army 104th Signal
Corps in Europe, whose motto "Get
the message through" saved thousands
of lives and battles from being lost.

ROBERT FOGATA, WORLD WAR II.
He enlisted in the army, was shipped overseas to Europe, and was in France in late 1943 with a special unit gathering information prior to the Normandy landing. He was in Rome in June 1944, and he recalled that when General Patton's Third Army tanks roared in, there were a few weeks of very heavy fighting.

JOE VILLA II, WORLD WAR II.
Joe Villa served in the U.S. Army during the Second World War.

JOHN SALAS, WORLD WAR II. Planning to serve in the Army Air Corps, after basic training Salas was returning home on furlough to see his fiancée. En route, he was killed in an automobile accident.

WHO KNEW IN 1946? Two friendly young ladies are entertaining two sailors at the Lakewood Country Club USO in Long Beach. From left to right are Barbara Marshall, two unidentified, and Ed Roina. Some time later, Barbara and Ed were married. She was a native daughter, and they moved to Santa Paula, where he headed the high school's music department for years; his jazz band was especially popular.

GATEWAY TO INCHON. Located near Seoul, this port city was the site of a key Korean Conflict battle, and once secured, it became a major entry point for troops. Thousands passed under this gate.

SAM SALAS. Upon returning from Korea, he assumed management of his family's Main Street business, the El Brillante Market.

DELTON LEE JOHNSON, KOREAN CONFLICT. Corpsman Johnson served on the USS *Haven*.

USS HAVEN. With the outbreak of the Korean Conflict, hospital ships such as this were desperately needed. With a capacity to accommodate 800 wounded, she served four tours in Korea and received nine battle stars.

HERMAN VILLA, KOREAN CONFLICT. Army Private Villa was killed in action in June 1952.

MANUAL ADAME, KOREAN CONFLICT. As a member of the army, Adame is standing at the far left with a part of his squad. He remembers no names because he was sent to Japan and never returned to his unit.

CAMP STONEMAN BUDDIES, KOREAN CONFLICT. This photograph was taken the night before the soldiers shipped out. The four men on the left were friends from Santa Paula; from left to right are John Godina, Mike Gaxola, David Lopez, Hector Borrego, and John ?.

TAKESHI CHIDA, 1952, KOREAN CONFLICT. This photograph was taken when the army staff sergeant returned home. Chida poses with his family while standing next to his brother, Tokio. Seated from left to right are his sister Sachiko Chida Ibusuki holding her baby John, mother Koto, father Yasuo, and brother-in-law Roy Ibusuki with his son Gary.

EDDIE BUSTAMANTE, KOREAN CONFLICT. Bustamante was a lance corporal technician 3rd grade in the U.S. Coast Guard from 1958 to 1960.

HENRY NAVA, 1948 TO 1954. He was a professional musician who played in the Marine Band. This photograph was taken on Treasure Island in San Francisco. Nava stands second to the right of the conductor, holding his clarinet.

ARTHUR TAPIA RABAGO (LEFT), KOREAN CONFLICT. Corporal Rabago wrote his own caption, "R & R to Tokyo, 2 females and a friend from Texas." Enlisted in 1950 in the National Guard, as a Ranger, he was assigned to intelligence training and deployed to Germany in 1951. He served in Japan and Korea, where he was mainly associated with the Far East Command Liaison Detachment. He made technician sergeant.

THEODORE RABAGO, KOREAN CONFLICT. He was killed in action in the Korean Conflict. His brother Arthur was flown from Germany to Oakland to escort the coffin home. Because there were few flights going west, he was put on any aircraft going in that direction. "Several times they tried to bump me but when they saw my orders" Arthur was allowed to continue. His brother was buried with full military honors in the Santa Paula Cemetery.

S.Sgt. Cecilio Huerta Preciado. It was during the Korean Conflict, but he was sent to Europe. Preciado went first to England and then to Germany, where he served in the Regimental Security Platoon, Division Headquarters of the Military Police from 1951 to 1953.

Pedro "Benny" Leon Jr., 1954. Pictured here at navy boot camp, Leon is depicted on the left.

Nine

PARTIES, PARADES, AND PLEASING PURSUITS

RUTH REDDICK'S BIRTHDAY PARTY, 1930S. From left to right are Caroline Bramesberger, Virginia Mac Murray, Mary Louise Call, ? Belin, Mary Strictland, unknown, Helen Gene Mac, Dick Dodds, Virginia Hardison, Barry Baumgartner, Ruth Reddick, Johnny Bramesberger (seated), Bob Reddick, Roy Wilson Jr., Tommy Wilson, Harry Reddick, Allen Hardison, Laura and Ann Gardner, Betty Wilson, and Dorothy Hedrick.

GOING BACK TO SCHOOL DAYS, 1947. Members of the IBC Club's Chapter 23 enjoy a picnic in Steckel Park, dressing as the theme suggested. Wearing their grammar school grins are, from left to right, Lottie Whidden, Myrtle Crumerine, and Mary ("Molly") Lidamore. (The meaning of the acronym IBC is known only to its members.) (Photograph courtesy of John Nichols Gallery.)

ELISEO SCHOOL ALUMNI, 1960. The one-room district school was located in Wheeler Canyon. From left to right are (first row) Francis Jauregui, Marie Jauregui Smith, Bob Jauregui, Lillian Jauregui Webber, Buddy Staben Jr., and Homer Bryson; (second row) Margaret Garmon, Bill Garmon, Catherine Jauregui Ellis, Annie Jauregui Yrigoyen, Anthony Jauregui, Jack Willett, and Bill O'Leary; (third row) Jauregui brothers Gracion, Pete, and Edward.

AN ANNUAL PICNIC, 1930. The Japanese lemon pickers and families who worked on the Limoneira Ranch every year gather together for a picnic. The caption for this photograph identifies the group as being the "Kumamoto people," meaning they were from that prefecture on Kyushu Island. It was loaned by Tokio Chida because even though his family and the Horitas lived and worked on the Teague-McKevett ranch, they were always included in the festivities.

THE FOURTH SATURDAY NIGHT BRIDGE CLUB. It started at the close of World War II and continued meeting monthly for more than 50 years. Replacements were made because of diminishing numbers. From left to right are (on the right side of the table) Elizabeth Blanchard (unfortunately partially hidden), Irv Wilde, Anita Tate, Fred Stewart, Phyllis Wilson, and Jack Samways; (in front) Delphine Wilde, Roy Wilson Jr., Theda Stewart, Eliot Blanchard, Evelyn Samways, and Eb Tate.

He Loved a Parade, 1940s. George Pezold, riding his handsome Arabian, had to trailer himself and horse to the nearby town of Ojai to participate in their festivities. Owner of the Santa Paula Super Market, he delighted in showmanship.

The 76 Union Oil Float, 1950. The company was born in Santa Paula in 1890, and some of the local employees went all out. The participants wore costumes befitting the various decades of the company's history. The names of all are unknown, probably much to their joy and enduring relief.

CITRUS WAS BIG IN 1952. The float passed by one of Santa Paula's half-dozen packinghouses then still in operation. As the recognized citrus capital of the world, local individual growers plus Limoneira's fruit were among the oldest and largest contributors to the success of the sponsor, the California Fruit Growers Exchange.

THE BUGGY IS ADORNED AND READY. The Limoneira Ranch sponsored an annual fiesta for the employees and their families. Everyone arrived in costumes. There were beauty contests, wonderful food, excellent music, and a moonlight dance. Here Leonardo Soto awaits the start of the parade with his colorful buggy.

HITCHED UP AND READY TO GO. Little Dolores Leon was playing with her baby brother Luis Jr. when a professional photographer happened by. Enraptured by the scene and the harnessed patient billy goat, he captured a very special moment.

A JEEP FULL OF SCOUTS, 1948. On the right side are, from left to right, Randy Fowkes, Grady Sewell, Phil Holts, and flag bearer Lee Hamrick. On the hood appears to be a large model glider.

MAIN STREET DUDES, 1951. For Fiesta Days, merchants and employees donned their Western garb. Shown here in front of Cauch's Drug Store are, from left to right, Hal Ringle, Jr. (owner's son), Ruth Edwards, Art Stuppy, Hal Ringle Sr. (owner), Annabelle Fuller, Annis Williams, Winnie Barger, and Walter Pendleton. (Photograph courtesy of John Nichols Gallery.)

MISS SANTA PAULA, 1961. Emma Navarro Romero was selected among the candidates to wear the crown after an hour-long program of modeling and judging in the high school auditorium. Her duties included welcoming visiting dignitaries, attending civic organization meetings, playing a prominent role in community Christmas activities, and competing for the Miss Ventura County Fair Queen.

115

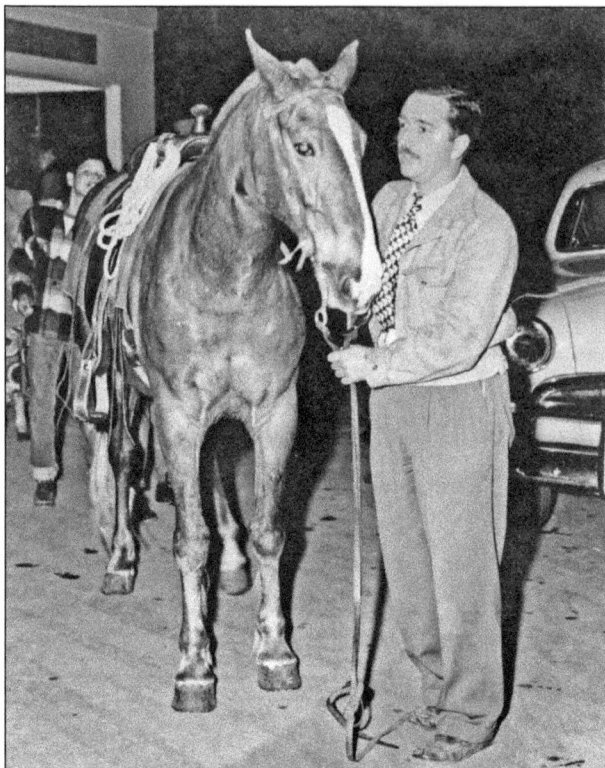

HE WON THE HORSE! Del King celebrated the grand opening of his Union 76 gas station with many prizes, including a horse with saddle. Tickets went like hotcakes, and a huge crowd gathered for the drawing. The winner was local merchant Bob Simmons, standing here with SPike—spelling intended. Unfortunately, he lived in town and had no corral. Eventually SPike went to Del King's daughter Sharon, whose grandfather was the manager of the Teague-McKevett Ranch and who did have a corral. SPike and Sharon lived happily ever after.

SANTA PAULA RODEO BILLBOARD, 1940. This was the second year that the Junior Chamber sponsored the rodeo to benefit the building of a clubhouse for the Boys Club and for developing playing fields for the community. It was also the year they celebrated and paid tribute to the Union Oil Company of California's 50th birthday. Festivities also included a Fiesta Days, parade, barbeque, Main Street sales, dances, and lots of hoopla. Cancelled during the war years, the popular event resumed in 1946 and continued into the 1950s.

CALF ROPING. Calf roping was just one of the events; among the others were bronc riding, Brahma bull riding, and steer wrestling. Professional riders and proficient wranglers came from far and near to compete for the purses. Bleachers to accommodate 9,000 spectators were built around the arena. The three-day shebang was held on the grounds of today's George Harding Park, so named to honor the man who spearheaded the annual benefit. Here Gracion Jauregui competes in the calf roping competition.

VISITING THEIR CONGRESSMAN, 1958. Republican Charles Teague was elected to the 84th Congressional District and remained in office for nine succeeding terms. He served from January 3, 1955, until his death January 1, 1974. Always the gracious host to any visiting constituents, here he poses with the Romney family. From left to right are Blaine, Phillip, Janette, the congressman, David, and Jeff.

DODGER BLUE, 1959. Boy Scout Kent Beckerdite and his troop pose with a real, live Dodger. The team had come to Los Angeles just two years earlier, so having a picture taken with a player made for a memorable scrapbook memento.

LOCAL WOODSMEN INSURANCE LODGE, 1952. A fraternal organization not just for woodworkers but also for any men seeking financial security through insurance, the national association was founded in 1890; now international, it continues to thrive. Luis Leon Sr. was a very active and vocal promoter of the group for many years.

BILL SAVIERS'S HOT ROD. It was a 1934 three-window Ford coupe with custom hood panels. To get just the right sheen, the beauty was given seven coats of black lacquer. Saviers commented, "Man, did it shine and did it show the dust!"

SNOW! By January 12, 1949, nearly 4 inches had fallen. Seventeen years had passed since the city's last snowstorm, so it is no wonder that the newspaper allowed, "Oldsters were amazed by the heavy downfall and youngsters were having the time of their lives playing in the precedent-breaking snowfall . . . drug stores report a run on picture film." These three photographs are a smattering of what the clicking Kodaks captured. With his artistic flare, Douglas Shively captured his snowed succulents.

FROSTY. The good chums standing with their creation are Dave Morua (left) and Harry Jue.

A PROFESSIONAL PHOTOGRAPHER'S TAKE. Shown is Dana Teague's photograph of his lemon grove and orchard heaters draped in white.

DUDE RANCH DREAM, 1940s. George Pezold, owner of the Santa Paula Super Market, also owned all or part of the Billiwhack Ranch in nearby Aliso Canyon. Born in Brooklyn, he came west as a young man and fell in love with the Wild West. The ranch inspired him to create a Western-style fantasyland for others to share and enjoy. This is a rendering of his planned resort with mechanical rides and lodging set in the wide-open spaces. Unfortunately, ill health robbed him of his visionary dream.

SS SANTA PAULA. This is the second Grace Line ship so christened. The first was a freighter commandeered by the navy to transport troops home after World War I. Sold, it was torpedoed in World War II. Built in the early 1930s, this luxury liner traveled from New York to South American ports. In 1958, a third one was built and sailed from New York around the Caribbean. It later became a hotel ship harbored in Kuwait, where it was sunk in the first Iraq War.

VIEW FROM A TOWER, 1937. The SS *Santa Paula II* was the first passenger ship out of San Francisco to pass under the just completed Golden Gate Bridge. A daring photographer memorialized the event. Specially designed for cruising the tropics by having only outside cabins, the *Santa Paula*'s outdoor tiled swimming pool was the largest saltwater plunge afloat at the time. The liner was one of 10 listed in a "Portfolio of Famous Ships."

A SECLUDED TREASURE. Once known as the Rancho del Oso Guest Ranch, it catered to a clientele who wished "to rest those jaded nerves." Built in 1930 and located on 160 acres, the accommodations were private cottages, cuisine included vegetables and fruit grown on the ranch, and there was horseback riding, swimming in the spring-fed pool, trout fishing, deer hunting, and golf or tennis privileges at the Ojai Valley Inn. Owned and operated by Mac and Mattie Harvey, pioneers both, the ranch was subdivided in 1969. It is now a private home.

EL RINCON, 1940s. In Spanish, El Rincon means "the corner," and to surfers it means great waves. To locals and those of neighboring Fillmore, having a beach cabin was heavenly in the summertime. However, the original owners bought lots near neighbors, so gradually two distinct neighborhoods or "colonies" developed. This is Dana Teague's off-shore photograph of the Santa Paula Colony.

HIGH SIERRA BASE CAMP. By the 1930s, some notable artists were calling Santa Paula home: Jesse Arms and Cornelis Botke and plein air painter Robert Clunie. Joining their company was a native son and aspiring plein air artist Doug Shively. Clunie spent summers at this spot, below the breathtaking Palisades Glaciers, capturing the magnificent scenery on canvas. Often the camp was shared by other artist friends or just families who liked to hike and fish and take in the camaraderie. This collection of photographs hints of those times.

ROBERT CLUNIE. The "Artist of the Palisades," his campsite was between the fourth and fifth lakes at 11,000 feet. Access to the area was limited, requiring miles of hiking. He had superb drawing abilities that gave his work a distinct, finished look; his paintings showed remarkable balance of design with strong values, bringing them alive with light.

A NOTED ARTIST VISITS. The man setting up the tripod is Edgar Payne, one of the most famous landscape painters and muralists of the West. He is preparing to take a photograph of members of the group in camp at the time, the Browns and Richardsons. Though not artists themselves, they were all old friends from Santa Paula.

JESSE ARMS AND CORNELIS BOTKE. Known for her white birds—pelicans, geese, ducks, cockatoos, and white peacocks—Jesse was considered one of the greatest decorative painters of the West. Her husband, Cornelis, also an artist, gained special recognition for his etchings. The two often collaborated on major works. For a holiday, they spent weeks at the Clunie camp painting, hiking, and enjoying nature.

ARTIST AT WORK.
Douglas Shively
studied with, worked
with, and relished
being with such plein
air artists as Paul
Lauritz, Robert Clunie,
John Cotton, and
Del Walker Warner.
Although he too
frequented the High
Sierra camp, here he
is busy painting at
some other location.

PAUL LAURITZ. Painting a scene in the golden hills of Santa Paula Canyon with his wife, Sylvia, looking on, Paul and the Shivelys were very good friends. Paul Lauritz was a versatile painter, and his diverse subjects included desert scenes, portraits, snow scenes, marines, and landscapes.

TENNIS JOCK, 1950. In his old painting pants and with a cigarette dangling, Ted Sharp serves up another ace. He was famous among his court pals for his vigorous playing and serving technique. Milton Teague hosted the standing matches at his ranch home. The other doubles players often included Robert Clunie, Roy Wilson Sr., Tom Rafferty, Howard Sheldon, and Harlow Atmore. For a change of pace, age, and looks, Agnes Pinkerton occasionally joined in.

LEADING THE CARAVAN, 1965. With flags flying, bands playing, officials smiling, and audience clapping, the first 13 miles of the 126 Freeway was opened. Leading the parade in a vintage auto are two local beauties, "Miss Santa Paula" Priscilla Pritchard and "Miss Ventura County" Cynthia Stocker. Joining in are official cars carrying local, county, state, and federal elected officials, all of whom helped officiate in the ribbon-cutting ceremony and congratulatory speeches.

Visit us at
arcadiapublishing.com